The Theater Goer's Dream

Rudolph M. De Leeuw

In the interest of creating a more extensive selection of rare historical book reprints, we have chosen to reproduce this title even though it may possibly have occasional imperfections such as missing and blurred pages, missing text, poor pictures, markings, dark backgrounds and other reproduction issues beyond our control. Because this work is culturally important, we have made it available as a part of our commitment to protecting, preserving and promoting the world's literature. Thank you for your understanding.

THE
Theatre Goer's
Dream.

—BY—

R. M. de LEEUW.

DEDICATED TO

Miss Clementine Albert.

NEW YORK:
Lowe & Co., Printers and Publishers, 210 Fulton Street.

1881.

Entered according to Act of Congress, in the year 1881,
—BY—
R. M. DE LEEUW,
In the office of the Librarian of Congress, at Washington.

IND FRIENDS:—

You will be surprised, no doubt, when I tell you that "My Awful Dad" has been informed by "The Professor," who is stopping at "Uncle Tom's Cabin," "The House That Jack Built," near "The Brook,'' that "The Danicheffs," "Man and Wife," after consulting "Our American Cousin," who was "Lost at Sea," have adopted "The Two Orphans," "Cris and Lena," who were brought here by "The Child Stealer of Paris," and whom they found wandering through "The Streets of New York," looking "Caste" down, standing here and there "Under the Gas Light" on "The Road to Ruin," asking charity "After Dark." It is their intention of placing these two children in the care of "Miss Multon," who will take them, under escort of "The Gladiator," to "East Lynne," and endeavor to instruct them, by the assistance of "Jane Eyre" and "Nicholas Nickleby," in the proper "School"—such is "The Lottery of Life."

After they are somewhat accomplished, "Billee Taylor" and "Enoch Arden"—a couple of "Our Boys" with "Hearts of Steele," and always "On Hand," will show them "The World—in fact, "Olivette"; and with "The Shaugraun" as valet, they expect to go "Around the

World in Eighty Days." The Captain of the "Pinafore," "A Rough Diamond," and husband of "Black Eyed Susan," has already, by the consent of "King Lear," offered them the freedom of his vessel with "The Royal Middy" as first mate, and assures his friends, "Virginius" and "Lady Clancarty," that during the voyage, he will wear the gift presented to him by Napoleon III., it being "The Legion of Honor," which he would not part with for any amount of "Money."

In his own language, which is to this effect— he said:—"We will go to 'The Islands in the 'Southern Seas,' where the 'Elfins and Mermaids' sport from morn till night, and on our return, after paying our compliments to 'Mary Stuart,' will, in around about way, visit 'Fritz in Ireland,' who had at one time, been 'Ten Nights' in a

Bar-room' under the influence of 'Drink,' and has now sown his 'Wild Oats,' by advice of 'Otto, a German,' who says it's 'Never too Late to Mend.'"

The Captain related a sad story of a man, named 'Ben McCullough," a relative of "The Danites," and one of "The Forty Thieves" who had jumped into the Sea; and from letters left to "The Pirates of Penzance," who are stopping at "Our Boarding House," we found it was "A Romance of a Poor Young Man."

"Camille," "A Child of the State," is supposed to have been the woman for whom this young man died. He had heard from "Miss Gwilt" that "Camille" and "Richelieu" were contemplating an elopement "Across the Continent" to the land of "Dixie," in "Pink Dominoes," and he, not desiring to experience any of the "Horrors" of a disappointment in love, thinking to avenge the perfidy of "Camille," committed suicide. "Effie Dean" says, it was "Love's Sacrifice"; I would term it "The Fool's Revenge." She, had a "Marble Heart," and it is the universal opinion, that after "The Long Strike," of which "Buffalo Bill" is the head, she will be "Condemned to Death"; for now the State, by order of "Louis XI.," have already placed her in the same prison, with "Rose Michel," who had been there "Almost a Life" (time), in charge of "The Three Guardsmen." If she should be placed on "Trial by Jury," it will really be "A Celebrated Case." "David Garrick" and "The

Lady of Lyons," "Bosom Friends"; People of the "Upper Crust," and of "Our First Families," with "Hearts of Oak, having heard of the "Prejudice" evinced toward "Camille" through a letter received from "The Wandering Jew," one of the "Exiles," have left their "Castles in Spain," where they are always protected "Under Two Flags," to pay "Camille" "A Morning Call." They are "Camille's" most staunch friends, and say that she is in "A Regular Fix," and does not make use of any "Diplomacy" for fear that "The Corsican Brothers," two "Bachelors," cousins of "Ours," who are all the time watching the hands go "Around the Clock," might say, "She Stoops to Conquer." That even in her present imprisonment, she still has brought to her daily by the niece of "Kit, the

Arkansas Traveler," " Esmerelda " from " Notre Dame," a " Forget Me Not " wrapped in " A Scrap of Paper," or some " Old Love Letters," found in " Bleak House.

Her cool behavior, under the most trying circumstances, is of such a nature, that " Don Cæsar de Bazaan," "The Liar," who is stopping with " The Serious Family " since the " Twelfth Night," styles it " London Assurance."

Even "The Hunchback," " The Black Crook," nephew of " Meg Merrilles," and a friend of " My Partner," in conversation at the House of "Widow Bedott," with "Jane Shore, Mary Warner and Henry Dunbar," whom we all remember— being the man rescued from " The Sea of Ice," by " A Woman of the People," from " Woodleigh," derided the action of " The Baffled

Beauty," and he said, "I thank Providence that "Oliver Twist" is yet a boy, or else he would have been a victim to this "False Friend's" charm, and "Led Astray," as were the "Troubadours," "The Rivals" of "Daniel Rochat" and "That Man from Cattaraugus," who formerly resided in the "French Flats" on "Fifth Avenue," with "A Gentleman from Nevada" and "Robert Macaire," wno is, by the way, endeavoring to find out "A New Way to Pay Old Debts."

"It is my candid opinion," said "The Galley Slave," "Formosa" to "Ingomar," "The Octoroon," who sat caressing "The White Fawn," that this meeting to gossip is a "School for Scandal," and I can say with a clear "Conscience," and without any "Risks," that in my opinion she is "Not Guilty."

I do not contend that she is "The New Magdalen," or that her principles are as good as are those of "Fernande" or "Frou-Frou," who are as innocent as "Babe's of the Wood"; but when "Little Nell,' as she was returning home from "Boarding School," through West Lane—the regular street being under repairs—and thus by that way there was "No Thoroughfare," laughing and chatting with "Fatinitza;" and she was stunned by that "Snow Ball" of hardened "Snow Flake," thrown from "Wolfert's Roost," by that "Grim Goblin," "Humpty-Dumpty" in one of his crazy "Freaks." Then for "Two Nights in Rome," "Camille" sat and nursed the child with that affection, which we experience daily between "Mother and Son." Now, that she is in trouble, as we were informed by "A Messenger from Jarvis Junction," who came here on "The Flying Scud," and her life at present to her is as dark as "An Arabian Night," would you have me display "False Shame," and act toward her "The Stranger? Let me tell you " Estelle "—in her youth, she lived in "The Gilded Age;" her days were passed as happy "Dreams," and had she never made the acquaintance of "Mazeppa" and "The French Spy," her life with the "Edgewood Folks," "Dora" and "My Son," would have been one continual "Enchantment." In consideration of the past, I would sacrifice considerable—"All for Her." Here you have "Rip Van Winkle," a regular "Nick of the Woods," whose wife, by advice of "Deacon Crankett," is seeking a "Divorce"—keeping company with

"The Crushed Tragedian," "To Oblige Benson," and carousing night after night "Ten Thousand Miles Away" from "Home," speaking of this poor unfortunate woman in prison, who played for "A Golden Game" in such a manner that the "Guv'nor" ought to send him on the Island, with "Robinson Crusoe" and "The Rag Picker of Paris," who looks just like the "Sphinx." This "Rip Van Winkle," so "Si Slocum," the brother-in-law of "Clarrissa Harlow," informs us, was married once before, and it was "Nora's Vow" (Nora being his first "Wife") that, according to "Article 47," if he ever married again, she would notify the "Captain of the Watch," and have him arrested by "The Little Detective" for "Bigamy," and thus "Rip" would experience that "Matrimony," although not "Forbidden

Fruit," was not to be trifled with, and that the "Marriage" to two or "One Hundred Wives," is held in our country in the same light, viz.: "Contempt of Court." And now "M'Liss" to hear any more aspersions against "Camille," I object—for, as "Kerry Gow" says, in her present predicament, she is worse off than "Leah, the Forsaken," for now she is "Twixt Axe and Crown."

Yesterday, while out shopping with "Evangeline" and Mrs. "Toodles," who had prevailed upon us to accompany her to "The Devil's Auction," we met "Romeo and Juliet," conversing with some of "Our Gentlemen Friends" from "Saratoga,"—and out of "Pique," as we passed them, we gave a cold salutation One of the gentlemen, as we got nearer to them, I perceived was "Unknown" to me. He was really handsome—looked like one of the old "Veterans"—and out of curiosity I waited at the opposite corner, as if for a car, until they should bid each other farewell. At last I was rewarded by "Ruy Blas" coming over and saying: "Well, dear! it seems "Ages Ago" since we met! Do you remember the time we had such "Fun in a Photograph Gallery." with the "Little Duke," who was having some "Photo's" taken, saying to each other, "Where's the Cat?" And you, by some mishap, lost your "Geneva Cross." I answered, yes, "Medea." Now, tell me who was that tall gentleman in your party?

That is "The Count of Monte Christo," "Engaged" to "The Lass o' Lowries. You have not the slightest idea "How She Loves Him," and she, was formerly "Yorick's Love." This is really a "Crabbed Age." Here are friends of "Kerry" from "Kennilworth," "Solon Shingle" and "Joshua Whitcomb," one of them a "Ticket of-Leave-Man," and both old cronies, with their "Hobbies," making love to "My Geraldine," and "Hiawatha." It is remarkable to see such "Old Heads and Young Hearts." Why, these two men are worse than "Box and Cox;" for if I had my way I'd have "Jack Sheppard" place them, without intending "Foul Play," "Neck and Neck" against a running pump; and if they were rescued by "Pomp" or "Sam," "The Belles of the Kitchen" and "Little Barefoot," "Nan, the Good for Nothing," might take them out in a row boat on a day when the Heaven's were full of

"Clouds" and mist, and thus have "Fun in a Fog."

These "Revels" would beat "Woodcock's Little Game," perpetrated on "Handy Andy" and "Jessie Brown," "The Irish Boy and the Yankee Girl," when he told them, that if they desired to fathom "The Mystery of Edwin Drood," it would be necessary to visit "Moses in Egypt," in company of "Jack and Gill," "The Emigrants"—each one of them wearing an "Iron Mask.

I suppose it a question with these old men, "To Marry or Not to Marry?" "Fanchon," the Cricket plagues them unmercifully, and last week when "Paul and Virginia," who are "Sweet Hearts," were on a visit, it was "A Terrible Temptation" to resist asking the old men out to play "Lawn

Tennis." But "Deborah," an "American Girl," who possesses "The Soul of an Actress," being present, refused to act in any way unladylike toward these old men, and tried to impress her young friends with "The Duke's Motto," which the friend of "Deborah," "Narcisse" thought was a most noble act. A peal of laughter rent the air, and we were pleased to receive "Cymbeline," "The Black Venus," who had just come in to say that she had an appointment at the ringing of "The Bells" with "The Merchant of Venice," and he had promised her an introduction to "The Tourists," "Ernani," "Powhattan" and "Ixion," whom they expected to meet in company with "Our Girls," at "The Mulligan Guard Silver Wedding." They, on their trip to Boston, had "Fun on the Bristol" with "Agnes"

"Evadne," "The Banker's Daughter," by placing on the sofas and chairs "Needles and Pins," and returned last Monday night with "The Colleen Bawn" and "Davy Crockett"—so I have been informed by "Sardanapolis"—to dine with "Hazel Kirke" at "Rosedale." By the way, "Hazel Kirke," whom "John Garth" says is "The Mascotte," has been circulating a report that the present management at the Madison Square think their play "All the Rage," and that they find "Millions in It." No one but "Fresh the American," whose sole ambition is to possess "The Mighty Dollar," would believe such.

"Pauline" says "Lord Dundreary" does not credit it, and in his letter from "Monte Carlo" to "Samuel of Posen," he says: "Such statements are only fit to be made to 'Cinderella at

School.' As to my own welfare, I had been a loser for some time, but now thank dame fortune that I have "Struck Oil," and "Won at Last.'"

When writing to Ohio, remember me kindly to "Our German Senator," who, when I was in politics, had always been "Our Candidate;" and also tell him to avoid the company of "Sharps and Flats."

It was a cool day in July, the same on which I saw "Julius Cæsar" assassinated, that I met "Hamlet," Prince of Denmark, at a reception given by "Othello" and his friend "Iago" to the "Merry Wives of Windsor." "Shylock" and "Richard III." had a discussion about a pound of flesh; "Henry VIII." came in while the discussion was in progress, and received from "Iago" the handkerchief which "Desdemona" had lost the evening previous. During the evening, "Richard III" proposed that they all go to the tower, to which they all assented. When they were safe in the tower, "A Tempest" came on, and "Antony and Cleopatra," to make the time agreeable, proceeded to give "Measure for Measure" and relate "A Winter's Tale."

Before they had hardly finished, "Macbeth" cried, "hold!—enough!" I would prefer seeing Richard II. go through the performance of "The Taming of the Shrew." "To my mind," said "Ophelia," "All's Well That Ends Well." But Macbeth, you are making "Much ado about Nothing." He answered, "As You Like It," and proceeded to inform "Ophelia" that the "Courtship between "Hamlet" and herself was "Love's Labour's Lost."

The "Two Gentlemen of Verona" and "Timon of Athens," having overheard the language used by Macbeth" toward "Ophelia," communicated the same to that noble Roman "Titus Andronicus," and he, to resent the insult of "Macbeth," promised to send "Pericles," Prince of Tyre, to King John, with information received, asking of "King John" to confer with "King Henry IV., and, if possible, secure the co-operation of "Troilus and Cressida" of Troy, and "Coriolanus" of Rome. That on the day when reparation is demanded of "Macbeth," the proper power may be brought to bear ; and thus by this unity of strength, there would be no possibility of a "Comedy of Errors."

This meeting of these great men of England, Greece and Rome, to be called into conference, that an uncouth man might be taught what is due to a noble woman, received the general approval of the populace, and night after night, "Rome in all its Glory," was made hideous by the rabble, who considered by the noisy demonstrations in which engaged, that this was the proper manner in which to display their approbation of the meeting of these great men.

It was on a July morning I woke up and found, to my dismay, that it was

"A Mid-Summer Night's Dream."

Printed by Libri Plureos GmbH in Hamburg, Germany